Adam said, 'Let's play doctors.'

1

Adam was the doctor.

This way up

Adam said,
'Let's play cowboys.'

5

He was the cowboy.

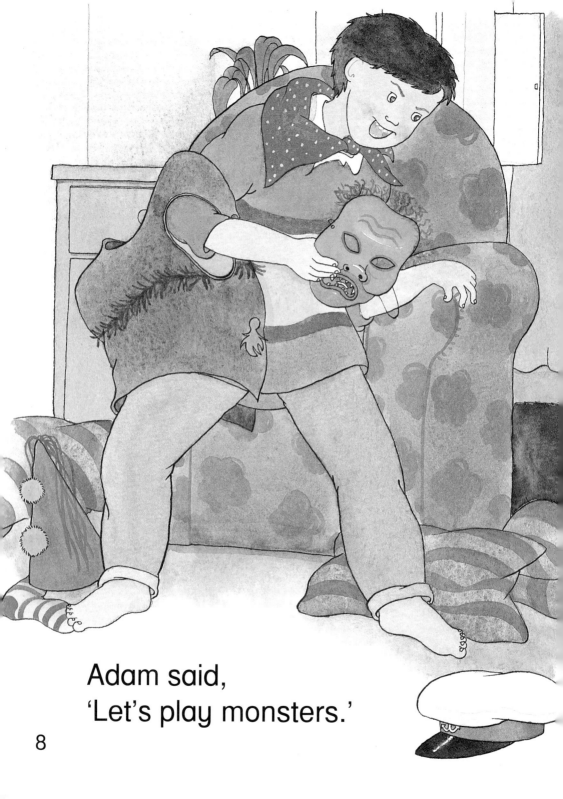

Adam said,
'Let's play monsters.'

He was the monster.

Sam was fed up.

This way up

Sam said,
'Let's play clowns.'

Sam was a clown.

Adam was a clown.

Splat!